Whispering Bones

Written with love by
Drew Hairgrove

"But you can choose to bury your past
in the garden by the tulips
water it until it's so alive
it lets you go
and you belong to yourself again."
-Andrea Gibson 'Royal Heart'

Dedication

To my mother, my momma, my tiki

As I'm sitting here trying to find the words to thank you, to tell you I love you and dedicate my first book to you, the only thing that comes to mind is my favorite memory of us. Remember seeing that snake in the backyard and how we purposely went and sat on the swing by it? Remember how we screamed and ran when it started coming towards us? Remember how we laughed so hard when we got to the safety of the porch? How silly we were to think that snake wouldn't chase us.

You are the porch in my life. So many times I have ventured out of the comfort and safety of your arms. No matter how many times life chased after me, you were always there for me to come home to: to find safety. You have always wiped my tears and said, "Go be young. Go live."

Because of you, I can.
I love you, my sky full of stars.

I am a petunia.

At first I fought hard for the burnt weeping blooms
to be mine forever
never to be trimmed.
But after many hot summer days
and the wind of a cold winter
I gave in and let go of my old faded beauty.
New fresh air has taken me places
I never would have imagined possible.
The petunia memories of my life
are the darkest
and the brightest.
I am a petunia.

Wendi J.

PART 1

"This part of my story is not a happy one, I know"
- Elizabeth Gilbert, *Eat Pray Love*

I gave you pieces of myself
that I borrowed from the future
And I'm not sure how to get them back
Without writing to the past.

$\mathscr{I}$ don't listen to music in the car anymore
I listen to poetry so loud
that the speakers go
bump bump bump
at all of the sad parts.
Today I saw a taxi driver cry as he checked the mail
and I wanted to stop and tell him that
some days I can't walk outside without crying either
and some days I feel like all I am is a taxi driver
escorting old loves to their true destiny.

The day you left I wiped my tears
on a white washcloth
and my mother kept it in her hope chest
so one day she can say,
"This. Remember this.
Remember how far you've come."
Sometimes I write about how you broke my heart
but I really think I'm writing
about how I broke my own heart.

I'm not angry at you.
I remember the years
that we danced by the water under the moonlight
But I missed you when I was next to you
and I missed you when you were in the other room.
We tried so hard to make our plans hold firm.

Some mornings the birds forget to sing
and the sun has to be reminded to rise and fall.
We set our clocks forward and back
to make up for the days
that the sun sleeps in or stays out past curfew.
Our sun may have set
but I can still feel the burn on my back.

$\mathcal{I}$ hope my moonlight catches your eye
as you're driving at night
and I hope your sun shines so bright on a new love.
I hope you found a way
to keep your tires from popping
and I hope you found a way to get better rest.
I hope the books on your shelf still excite you.
But mostly, I hope you make yourself proud.

Because you weren't proud of yourself
as you tucked me in all those nights.
Maybe because we ran into love full force
and I'm afraid a love like ours
is a one-shot kind of thing
but we fucked it up somewhere between
casseroles and planning a wedding
that I forgot to invite myself to.

And the years passed so quick, ya know?
We saved for used furniture,
we read cookbooks,
got excited over new kitchen appliances.
Your family gave us a vacuum for Christmas.
That was us though; simple and eager.

After all those years together
I cant remember
how your voice sounded saying my name.
Some days I wish I never met you,
Just so I could meet you tomorrow.

I wish I didn't grow old with you so young,
I wish I could have saved you for later.

March **4, 2013** I was unpacking when I heard you walk in. I had on light pink lipstick that I found at the bottom of a box. You put a few things on the counter and handed me my car keys. I kissed you and asked if you could help me move the bed. You said you needed to talk. I keep replaying this over and over in my mind. I don't think I'll be able to unpack the rest of these boxes .

April 4, 2013 It's been a month since you left. Mark says you're not coming back. I can't sleep. Are you awake?

June 4, 2013 I sold my engagement ring at a pawn shop today. I bought expensive lipstick and flowers. It's weird being back in this town without you. I spend most of my afternoons at the beach. I saw a sea turtle while I was swimming. I miss eating breakfast food at midnight with you.

July 4, 2013 I stumbled across a video of you singing in the car. I deleted it before it played all the way through but I have to admit it made me laugh. I broke down and called you. Thank you for not answering

August 4, 2013 I forgot all of the words to my favorite song when you drove past me today.

September 4, 2013 I went on a date. He thinks cheap beer is "quality beer". It just isn't going to work out.

October 4, 2013 It doesn't hurt to say your name anymore.

November 4, 2013 I hope you're doing well.

December 12, 2013 Thank you for setting me free.

March 4, 2014 It's been a year. I haven't heard anything about in you awhile. I don't know what you've heard about me but I hope it's that I'm happy. I hope you've heard from our friends that they often see me sitting in the sun, laughing with my hair in a braid, collecting seashells and running straight into the ocean with no fear.

This is not a broken love.

This is two people walking
One north
One south
This is not the end because we never really began
and I still see your car coming
down the road as I roll down the window for air.
This is not just a broken love

This is Russian Roulette
The "you're too young for love"
like bullets crucifying
me to a dream across state lines
and I have a confession:
Was it you?
You like a beacon
guiding me to a mistaken freedom,
like an escape to an unknown world
trying to devour my innocence
Or was it love?

This was a lie.
A beautiful fairytale folded over our eyes
as the angels and demons fought for our youth.
Your shirt hung off your body
like the lies that dripped from your teeth.
There was too much time
spent counting the seconds
that I never begged you stay
and fight for one more chance.
Because our chance wore thin
with talk of money
and our wants held tightly and clung for hope,
when hope held nothing but our broken destiny.

We wasted time.
Time planning for the future
and when the future stopped spinning
Its web of lies it was time for us to say,
"This is not a broken love."
I was a secondhand book thrown
from one heart to the next
where you picked me up
from a mud puddle.
I was another book for your collection,
another book you never took the time to read
but talked like you memorized the copyright.
This is not just a broken love.

This is a crack in my heart.
This is me pouring seeds into those cracks
hoping something beautiful blooms
without a trace of your name.

This is not a broken love.
This is not a beautiful poem
weaved and signed with my name,
exhaling the poison you soaked my heart in
leaving me with only a match to ingest.

This is not a history lesson punched with
red, white and blue for you to share
with your kids as you roll a cigarette.

This is Russian Roulette.
Drilled into the back of my thighs
is the apology that never came.

This is goodbye.
This is we tried.
This is roulette.

For awhile we lived in a tiny apartment with green carpet. The front porch light quit working after you tried to change the bulb. Our windows didn't lock all the way and the wall had a hole hidden behind a poster from where you punched it.

The first night we moved in, I cried. The only thing we had time to move after work was our mattress, sheets and pillows. I remember being curled up on the mattress in my work clothes, so tired and scared of our little apartment. It was so quiet. I could hear the crickets outside of our window, the rustle of the trees and a dog barking. It smelled like bleach and dust. You told me not to cry as you handed me one of your over-sized t-shirts to sleep in. You held me until I fell asleep.

You were so proud of that place. It was cheap and all we could barely afford but you were proud. I remember you trying to grow peas in a little plastic pot...gosh you were so cute. You'd come home and move them into the sun and water them with this smile on your face, this smile that stole my heart every time.

We would wake up early on Saturday mornings when we both didn't have to work and go buy flowers. We had a pink chair on the front porch and a bench...the 'Robert Bench', which was a large storage container that we sat on. My pink chair was stolen and you walked through the whole neighborhood trying to find it. You said, "Drew, it's your princess chair. I'll find it for you." You never found it but I was happy siting on that storage container just to enjoy coffee with you in the mornings.

The day I moved back to our hometown for my medical appointments, we packed my things into my old, red car . You promised me you would take care of the rest of the apartment and come home to me. But you never came home.

Some nights I wonder about that apartment. I wonder why we never got a goodbye, why I ended up selling my engagement ring at a pawnshop. I wonder about the next girl you brought to that apartment. I wonder if she ever noticed the little things about you that I loved. Like how you enjoyed watering your plans when you got home from work, how you face the shower head to wash your hair, how you keep track of how much change you have down to the pennies.

I wonder if you ever looked at her
and just for a second
wished it was still
me.

$\mathcal{I}$ packed up my past in the
biggest bag I could find
without bothering to tie it shut.
I didn't donate the good memories
to the sleepy voice of
'I miss you'
I didn't recycle the whispered
'I love you'
I didn't return the kisses that I had no time to use.
I didn't care.

I just drove.
Drove anywhere that I didn't see your face.
The ocean crashed against
the shore in the rhythm of,
"Who are you now?"
I didn't care.

I typed my words night after night,
words I knew you'd never see,
a broken letter sent to the deepest grave.
I bled onto a blank page to
make sense of our goodbye.
I bought two journals hoping
it would be enough to say
I don't care.

I wrote until every line turned
into a sloppy love story
told backwards.
I wrote until my eyes blurred.
I didn't care.

I stopped holding on to you.
I stopped trying to fill the hole
you punched into my heart.
The sad words quit flowing from my pen.
I woke up this morning and I cared.
I cared about me.

In order to let you go I went back
to the places that I gave you a piece of my heart.
Not because I wanted those pieces back
but because I needed to remind myself
that we really happened,
that we weren't always
the broken wreck that we turned into.

But the one place that I couldn't go
existed in our twisted world
that quietly slipped out the back door;
vandalized
condemned
beaten
covered in vines
and swallowed by the sea.

You'll look back one day.
You'll search for that place just as I did.
You'll show up at my doorstep,
see my smile and painfully realize
that someone planted wildflowers
in the cracks you left in my heart.

My love isn't yours anymore.

*I*t was over
just like that.
I didn't say anything except
goodbye
But what I really wanted to say was
I'm sorry.
I'm sorry if my love wasn't enough.
If I could go back and take mornings off
so we wake up early and garden,
I would.
I'm sorry for all the times
I kept you up late
talking to the ceiling.
I'm sorry I never made your coffee right
...two tablespoons of sugar,
not one
and never three.
(I'm sorry for that)
But most of all,
I'm sorry for all the times I let you down.
I just thought the one day you let me down
would be when you forgot our dinner date

Not our love.

I can't recall when the heat took over.
I don't remember the chilled air leaving
or the smell of the fire dwindling.
But one day winter was gone
and so were you.
(how quietly it all slipped out the back door)

$\mathcal{I}$ had a dream that I died last night.
I waited for my life to flash before my eyes.
I saw your face instead.
Once when we met.
Twice us laughing in your car.
Third your mouth saying,
"It wasn't love."
"It wasn't love."
"It wasn't love."
But I wondered how I could die twice:
Once when you broke my heart.
Twice when my broken heart stopped beating.
(how dare you be there for both)

$\mathcal{I}$ was notch number four on your bedpost.
You were notch number one on mine.
Except I never carved your name.
You meant more to me than
a tally mark
on a bedpost
that knocked a hole straight through my heart.

I opened the window today
and closed my eyes.
It's fall now.
Fall always felt like our season,
I wish I would have told you that.
I felt the wind blow in our memories,
memories I've been trying to forget.

This wasn't how our story
was supposed to end, was it?

Did our story end
or did we just set down the book for a little while?

And I've wondered three times on my back
if the twenties in your wallet
still beat against your hip bones
like my lips did on your neck.
And I've counted the pillows on my bed
like I've counted the seconds
until the alarm clock of our love just
....went off.

And I think there is something to be said
for the way I've let you go.
I can't be the queen bee
in the face of heartache anymore.
I can't keep drawing cracks on the cards
with hearts on them
and I can't keep dealing myself a new hand,
hoping life passes me the winning number
for the game called
love.

I've spent 1,3777 minutes
spelling your name backwards,
hoping that I can make sense of our past.
but each letter only spelled out
the days I've wasted trying to forget you.

You sewed your kiss into my ribs
many moons ago
and I finally found a way
to untie
each
broken
promise.

$\mathscr{A}$fter you left I had to learn how to say my name without yours behind it. I repeated my name over and over. It was never 'where are *you* at?' it was always 'where are *ya'll* at?' It was always us walking through a grocery store at midnight or racing up the stairs to see who could get to my bed first. It was always us taking a shower at the same time, one of us shaking in the cold while waiting for our turn under the hot water. It was always me laughing into your neck. It was always you.

After you left I didn't know if I liked cream in my coffee or if I drank my coffee black. Hell, I didn't know if I even liked coffee at all. After you left I couldn't remember which toothbrush was mine, if that was your sweater or did I own it the whole time?

After you left I tried to remember what I did in my spare time. My hands kept reaching for the phone to see when you were getting off work or if you could stop and pick up beer on the way home. I wanted to call and ask what you wanted for dinner. (I wish I would have cooked for you more.)

After you left I looked in the mirror for a long time. My hair was so short I couldn't put it up and my face was so round from circling my mind...but I never cried. I never cried until ten months passed and our anniversary punched the calendar. I sat outside with my knees to my chest in my parent's driveway. I sat in the same spot we used to when we were just two kids in high school falling in love. The same spot I'd sneak out and meet you with cookies.

You know, I doubt you even realized it had been twelve months since you heard my voice. I doubt you even realized how different your name sounds without mine flowing behind it.

Some days your love felt like sleeping with too many blankets, like waking up hot and annoyed. Some days your love felt like the cool air across my body when I kicked off the blankets and rolled over.

Some days your love felt like sweeping carpet with a broom, like I swept our green carpet over and over and over, knowing a vacuum would be easier. Some days your love felt like I was the carpet and you just walked over me, wiping the dirt off your shoes onto my back.

Some days your love felt like winter and coffee; safe and warm. Some days your love felt like kissing your chest while slipping a piece of dark chocolate into your back pocket. Some days your love felt like my favorite holiday that I got to enjoy every day.

Towards the end your love felt sad, not because you forgot to love me back but because I realized I was losing you to the passing seasons. Some days your love made me feel like I was the last leaf to fall as I watched your colors change and fade without me.

Towards the end your love felt like taking a hot shower and shivering under the air vent when I realized I forgot a towel.

*D*ear you,

It's October again, the year has come full circle. To be honest, it has always felt like October when your name crosses my mind. Tonight I was driving home from my parent's house and thought of you. It's the first cold night of the season. I felt like I was driving home to something unknown because this time last year I would have been driving home to you. I have all of these things to tell you; souvenirs that I've compiled on my journey without you, things I know you would find interesting. I don't where your mailbox is anymore but I hope one day this finds you well.

Things change, ya know? We used to talk about how everything seemed to change but us, little did we know we were changing the most. I look over and you aren't in the chair next to me and that car coming around the corner isn't yours. I tell myself goodnight now, in a king size bed all alone. But these changes....they are okay. I just wish we weren't so foolish to think that we were the one exception.

We were young but our love was real, there is no denying it. We never went to New York to drink cold beer in the snow and we never completed the list you kept in your glove box. That wedding book you bought me ended up in the dumpster. I was going to marry you, remember? But all of this doesn't make us bad people. What you did doesn't make you a bad person and how I reacted doesn't make me selfish. What makes us feel a bit of guilt is that we chose to ignore that we were changing; we believed that love will always be enough. But it's not, it never will be for anyone. We are just people floating in and out of each other's lives and that little bit of time has to be enough.

I want you to know that I forgive you. I want you to know that I am thankful for the years spent by your side, for the history lessons and late night cigarettes, for the adventures. We had some damn good times together.

I want you to know that I forgive you,
Please understand this.
I want you to know that I will always remember you on these October nights.

(even though it always feel like October when you cross my mind.)

Cheers,
Drew

Whispering Bones

PART 2

"The time has come," the Walrus said.
-*Alice in Wonderland*

You remind me of a summer night.
You seem so endless,
But I know you will come to an end
Before I'm ready to say goodbye

Whispering Bones

I was making strawberry cupcakes
when I realized that I can't rhyme.
I wrote poems in pink gel pen on my thighs;
I spent a year writing the same poem
over and over and over.
you carved lines across your thighs
a year before you met me.

It was a cold December night
when you took your pants off in front of me,
I was sitting at the end of your bed and thought,
"Oh my gosh. Did he just do that?!"
but what fell out of my mouth was,
"...your balls are bigger than I expected.
I mean...wow. You've got big balls.
No, that doesn't sound right either....
What I'm trying to say is you're brave."
You laughed and said,
"Let me show you my twisted art."
My fingers traced the scars along your thighs
like crossing a railroad track.
I had nothing to show,
the gel pen poems had faded
so I pulled you close
and fell in love with your sadness.

I used your scars as stems
and drew gardens up your body.
I bought a notebook and tried to rhyme.
But what word rhymes with orange?
if orange can't rhyme then I don't want to either.
What word rhymes with growing old too fast?

What word rhymes with falling out of love?

Some days I don't know how to feel whole anymore. I don't know how to shake a stranger's hand without slipping a note in their palm before I walk away. I don't know how to look in the mirror and say, "You belong to yourself. This is you. These hands are yours. This battle...it's yours."

I hear silverware dropping as I stir cream in my coffee and I hear rain crying against my window on the sunniest of days. I love and love, writing about heartache while I myself have broken hearts in the dead of night. I don't know how to take this pain and hold it in my hands long enough to grasp it, to own it, to make it right.

I make my bed in the morning to the hum of regret and hang pearls on the skeletons in my closet. I kick stilettos off after a long day and let my hair fall to my shoulders as I wipe red lipstick on the back of my hand. This year has fucked me night after night and I'm too weak to say no.

But now I grasp a stranger's hand and kiss their cheek, shaking my happiness into their life. Smile, laugh, make these memories and run. Please don't stop running until you can look at yourself in the mirror with comfort. Don't stop running until you are strong enough to bury the skeletons in your closet during the midnight hours. Don't stop running until you can exhale a sigh of relief over a cup of coffee and say,

"This battle...it's mine."

$\mathcal{I}$ve seen my name spelled five different ways,
all traced across my chest like tiny candles
illuminating each letter.

I've encountered love resting in my bed.
I've watched it with eyes closed
and grew jealous of its clean conscious
and slow breathing.
I tallied the days I spent loved
but not in love.

I drank six beers to remember that
days can map out the way from my house to yours
but I wasn't sober enough
to say your name next to mine.

With eyes closed I saw an open casket
at a funeral that I forgot to attend
because I buried my heartbreak
so many months ago.

I have fallen into routine and my bones hurt from waking in this southern heat. I come home from work and just want to take off this dress, this heavy jewelry. I want to take off my armor and just be small.

I'm pacing, literally pacing my cold floors with no shoes on. I'm walking circles thinking 'maybe I should make my bed with the white sheets next time, maybe that dress needs to be ironed. If I had a ladder I'd hang those curtains back up, maybe I should repaint these walls.'

There are three glasses of sweet tea on my coffee table. The ice has melted and I pour another glass. I think my phone is ringing but I'm so sick of talking, so sick of pushing little letter messages. I want ink stains on my hands. I continue pacing while saying this out loud. I've been pacing for ten months, pacing the same floors I used to sit and laugh on.

My mom told me I should keep writing. I want to tell her it hurts to relive so many of my memories. She says she's proud of me; that I've come so far. I'm not sure how to tell her that I'm still walking in circles waiting for someone to tell me

'Stop.
Just rest.
Breathe.
Let me pace for you.
Rest.'

And I can't remember if it was you or I who put sugar on their toast but I think it was I who said,
"If I ever leave,
I swear you'll find a way
To stay afloat."

$\mathcal{I}$ wish I could cry.
The only tears I know are words on paper,
salt down my cheek has become foreign to me.
I sleep with my fan on high and the heater on.
I can't figure out everything at once
and when you ask me who I am
I want to draw tiny cherry blossoms
on your wrists,
leave the taste of brown sugar on your palms,
mix pink and red carnations in a vase,
hang Christmas lights in the summer,
wake with the sun
and fall asleep under a down comforter.
I want to tell you that there is too much
of me to learn in a night
and I know you've got no time
to ask why I can't cry.
So when you asked who I am
I replied quickly with,
"A mason jar of sweet tea."
but I could tell by the look on your face
that you have no idea what that means:

Sweet, simple and southern.
mix with lemons or berries.
I haven't the slightest idea
how to quench your thirst
when sugar is the only substance I know.
my words
water down
every
piece
of
me

You spent six months wondering if it was your fault. No, it wasn't. It never was. I know you're tired of telling yourself goodnight and buying flowers to put on your coffee table to feel special. It's scary to let someone in when the fence you've built around your heart just started to grow jasmine and you were about to paint that fence pink. If you like it there, you don't have to knock it down; just let him talk to you through it for awhile.

I know you're waiting for someone to ask you deep questions that are meaningful. You're a hopeless romantic, you're waiting for the movie love; anything short of that and you are disappointed.

If I could find someone that can look past your blue eyes and yearn to know everything about you, I think you might feel a little more at home. But you don't know where home is and a man won't help you find it.

So go paint the fence around your heart pink and tell yourself that you are beautiful as you fall asleep. Because you spent six months wondering if it was your fault and I won't let you spend another day wondering if you are someone's first thought in the morning. You are mine and mine you will be until a man is willing to cross the universe for you. That's what you deserve.

You begged me to love you,
I looked at you with twisted eyes as I whispered,
"You don't want this poison."
you took five steps forward
and five steps back.
You don't want this poison.

My pockets were filled with pennies
that I collected when
you asked if it was time.
But the clock on the wall stopped ticking
and I never meant to have this much change.
The pay phone kept ringing
and you kept asking
and I said calmly,
"You don't want this poison."

Because sunsets and coffee
aren't enough for me.
I looked at love as a bouquet of daggers,
you looked at love with a light in your eyes,
begging to feel it.

I needed a man who was already broken,
someone who had already stitched
the pieces of his heart back together.
I needed a man who had lost love once
and was ready to try again
one last time.

A girl like me will destroy you.
You don't want this poison.

You probably shouldn't love me. My tears will hit your thighs like acid rain and my journal will be the thing you can't touch. You can read my words in braille on my back and I will whisper them into your mouth but the words on paper are my past. Showing you these thoughts would be like opening pandora's box and you will see nothing but disappointment.

You probably shouldn't love me, even though I'm easy to love. You can take me around town and hold my hand under the stars while we look to the moon, but my mind will race with words to describe the scene and you'll have to repeat everything two times just to make sure I heard you over my own thoughts.

You can kiss me here and there and I'll promise you coffee and late nights but my hands will etch sentences into the sheets until I find my way back to pen and paper.

You probably shouldn't love me unless you don't mind sharing me with my writing. You may have to remind me to drink more water and tell me to slow down when my thoughts race too fast. But one day I'll hand you the paper and pen, and in your hands my heart will rest when my timid thoughts let you see me write down these words.

You probably shouldn't love me,
but would you?

Would you notice when she's sad
Or wonder where she's at?
Do you know that she never
finishes a cup of coffee
and she hates french vanilla creamer?
Do you tell her goodnight
without a rush in your voice?
Or silently think about her
when you're busy?
Did you spend an hour after that first kiss
wondering if it was cherry or strawberry
you tasted?
I'm sure you've asked what she's scared of
and why she sleeps with so many blankets,
and you know that her hair
smells like coconuts
And if she lets you know she cries,
she loves you.
You know this right?

Do you love her like she deserves?
Do you love her like she deserves?

Because the clock in my head strikes
midnight at 9:45
and with each
Click
Click
Click
of my keyboard I remind myself
that she is proud of me.

An inspiration, she says.
A writer.
A poet.
I'm so sick of words clouding my vision.
I want to tell her this.

My past is growing thicker with fog
and I hardly remember the person I used to be.
I don't want you to remind me
and please don't say you loved me.
She is proud of me.
I wish she could tell me who I am.

You are cracked hip bones
sealed with pink glue.
You are cherry lip gloss.
You are cracked hip bones
sealed with pink glue.
You are cracked hip bones.

There's nothing poetic about me,
not really.

But I think everyone can relate to something
once broken.

I know you think this town
is too small for the both of you.
One day you will be out with friends
and see him by coincidence,
your heart will skip a beat,
that smile will bring back old memories.
Look, I know you will
want to push your lips against his
and sit down at the bar next to him
to take a shot.
You'll want to ask how he's been.
But don't.

Listen, I know you quit smoking
and late at night you
want to light one up to feel him in your lungs.
and I know your favorite song comes on
and you feel his arms around you
and want to pick up the phone
but don't.

You were a stop on a long road trip.
You were the best beer he ever had
that gave him the worst hangover.
You are the bittersweet comfort of the past
and darling, there is no room in the future.
Don't.

You aren't eighteen and stupid anymore.
You aren't the windows down
and a bottle of cheap vodka.
She must he his favorite beer now,
but you,
you were his hardest goodbye.
Don't.

I have seen good people lullaby
themselves to sleep with a smile
and wake to the temptations of this world.

I have seen darkness slice skin one cut too deep like a fire that crushes whole dreams. I have seen the ash of innocence fall from the ceiling fan when good people relish in deceit. Sometimes there is nothing left but a quick sentence that whispers all but an apology.

I have seen a shell of a person with weak knees bend down for a penny on the ground. I have seen good people stray down a path they can't fight on their own. I tore down the hopes for you and carried them on my back. I carried the burden for the both of us; your guilt weighed heavy on my spine and cracked my ribs.

But I guess that's how the straw that broke the camel's back felt; like a light weight object free falling towards a desert monster until even the slightest wind could tip over the Eiffel Tower.

You were the wind.
I was the Eiffel Tower.

I have seen goodbye lullaby
themselves to sleep with a smile
and wake to the temptations of this world.

Nostalgia

The rush of you driving your car too fast,
the music loud and windows down.
cheap beer and limes,
daydreaming of coconuts and pink umbrellas.
How the smell of cigarettes lingered
on nights we would soon regret
the mistakes we made with boys
who claimed to love us.
Up the stairs and to the right
Up the stairs and to the right.
The way your house was so still
after Penelope died.

I'm sorry that I left you
to chase a Mississippi sunset.
I should have been laughing
with you all along.

Nostalgia.

Nostalgia II

It was never my dream I was following,
It was two years spent in confusion.
The only thing that made sense was you.
Running up the stairs laughing,
the scent of pine tress in our kitchen.
Late nights by the fire,
our secrets slowly burning
with each broken branch.
Two knocks on the wall,
my room to yours.
Beer cans decorating our back porch
on the sunny days
when we should have been in class.

I'm sorry I left you to chase a Florida sunrise
But it was time for me to go home.

Nostalgia.

How to heal from a breakup:

My only advice is to make your life beautiful in your eyes.

Stock your fridge with colorful fruit and spend an hour picking out flowers for yourself. Buy lace curtains and sit in the sun. Have a cup of coffee and just write. Write anything. Write the alphabet in cursive.

Go buy new sheets, the light pink ones with the ruffles. You deserve it. Take a shower every night before bed and use hibiscus soap. Laugh at how he would have hated pink sheets. This is your bed now. Tell yourself goodnight with kindness and sincerity.

Spend $80 on that perfume you've always wanted. Throw away all the others and while you're at it go buy those earrings.

Go back to school and learn. Buy expensive notebooks and tie your hair back with pink ribbons. Don't wait for a man to buy you that diamond bracelet. Work hard. Get a job you love.

Stock up on clean linen candles and keep one burning at night while you are reading. Read something good, this is important. Read until you fall asleep with the book in your hands. I forbid you from reading romance novels.

Take all the love you had for him and give it to yourself. You never stop loving that person, you just stop giving your love to someone who isn't there anymore. Take care of you. One day you'll wake up to the sun shining through your window and your hair will lay across a pink pillow and you'll smile. All of those days you spent crying will seem so distant. You'll be okay. I promise.

$\mathscr{I}$ loved with innocence.

But innocence make you woozy
like five beers
and innocence is bittersweet
like a hangover-
we had fun
and paid the consequences.
Love lost.
Innocence fades.

I took a writing class
And the instructor said my words
read like painting.
I took a painting class
and the instructor said my paintings
swirled like poetry.
Everything I created whispered your name;
a testimony that my fragile wrists
could make our war of a love
look so damn beautiful.

But you'd laugh because
you know I never could keep my hands
steady enough to paint you out of the picture.

But you'd laugh because
you know I never had my shit
well enough
together to make anything beautiful
on purpose.

When she asked what kind of love inspired me to paint cherry blossom trees instead of weeping willows I said, "The kind of love that blooms so quick and delicately that by the time you get your camera, the petals have already fallen."

When they ask why I don't write
about pure love and candy
I ask why they don't visit their grandparents more,
put more in the offering plate at church,
call their mother just to say goodnight.
There are some things we should do
but just don't.

There are some things we wish we could change
but just can't.
I write for reasons like this.

Some people just can't date writers.

There are some people who will be fascinated by the way you string words together, how you find beauty in the girl who lost her hat to the wind at the park, how you hand write every letter and mark the sad parts with tears, how you close the envelope with ink stained wrists.

But there are some people who will look at you like you have lost your damn marbles. There are some people who will lose patience in your bedside lamp turning on and off late at night as you scribble words on the back of a receipt. There are some people who will trip over your crumbled papers and chewed pens with a sigh of annoyance. These people will take you by the hands and say,
"Damnit.
Can't you just drink the coffee without trying to write a love letter with the cream and sugar?!"

Some people just can't date writers.
Most people don't deserve to.

My darling, my dear, this isn't new to you. Tell me how many nights you have lined your eyes with black. Tell me how many times you have looked in the mirror trying not to cry.

My darling, my dear, this isn't new to you. You may look different from when he loved you; your waist now smaller and hair longer but the way you always step with your right foot first gives you away and you can't hide that smile.

My darling, my dear, this isn't new to you. He keeps his house cold and it smells like fall and you spend nights sitting outside planning your new life. The truth is, this boy doesn't make your heart beat fast like his did.

So you go home and twist the tops off of mason jars and sip out of a pink straw. My darling, my dear, this isn't new to you. You chased him to love you and you chased him to leave you. And maybe he still sits outside, lighting his cigarette with the flame of your past and I bet he whispers your name.

I bet he whispers your name.
Let go.

You asked me why the flowers in the vase
  don't need sunlight
  and were disappointed when I told you
  It was because they are already dying.
  I've never felt more like
  a carnation in a mason jar of water.

This is the only way I know how to say
that I'm sorry for still writing about you,
that I'm still pushing flowers into the sunlight,
still buying packages of salted sunflower seeds
and planting them in my garden,
still plugging in Christmas lights with blown bulbs.
evidently I don't let go of things as easily as you.

My mom told me you know you're over it
when you become empathetic.
When I began writing,
I would read her little paragraphs nervously
and she'd say,
"You didn't write that..."
while kissing my cheeks
as I swore that I did.
Evidently it's not normal to feel life so hard.

If you ever want to know what it felt like
to sit on the pier without you
remember the flowers in the vase,
remember how they are dying so beautifully
just for your pleasure.

I wasn't always an apology that you'll never read.

There's more to me than I let on. I'm not a writer, not really. I have no secrets. You can ask me anything and I'll tell you. I have hardly any self-confidence and I know apparently self-confidence is sexy but I'm not that either. I'm nervous. I'm "cute". I'm the girl who reads in class. Sometimes I forget to eat and my hands shake when I paint or meet new people or go to the mall alone. Dammit, I'm more than a pretty face. I'm smart and independent. I read books about dead writers and trace their words in cursive. I'm timid and scared. I'm scared of everything. I just want to feel special and important. I wear my innocence like a diamond necklace that I refuse to take off even though I can't afford it.

Please don't take it from me.

Things aren't always going to be easy.

When you are in the sixth grade you will meet your sister for the first time, that night you will have to escape the beating on the door. You'll be okay. Don't be scared.

When you turn 15 you'll meet him. Two months later you will give him everything. It's not beautiful. Don't fool yourself.

Look, you are going to pack up and move but you won't be happy when you get there, not really. Call your mom and tell her you love her (and don't sign that second lease).

Don't marry him. He's not the one. Listen to your heart when you make the guest list and forget to include yourself: That sick feeling won't be nerves. Run, you'll want to. Do it.

My girl, you are beautiful. Don't spend those years pushing down on your bones. Be gentle to your body. When you are 20 you will fall in love with yourself. I promise.

Please listen to me. When he says he doesn't know why he loves you, walk away. That boy only loves the way your body curves around his.

Don't stop writing. One day you will get the courage to share your words. You'll regret ripping the pages out of your journal. Don't listen to him when he says he doesn't understand why you want to write everything down.

And I know you won't understand this..

But the guy who drives the jeep, he'll kiss you on the beach. Please tell him not to give up. You may just save a life.

Who taught you
to be so frail
when your bones
were made to
hold your strength
refusing to break

I was buying strawberries when I got lost in thought
staring at the lilies and hydrangeas by the check out.
This man walked up to me and said,
"I've never seen anything more beautiful."
"Flowers are poetic," I thought.
But you can't tell people these things
so I smiled and looked away.

I used to carry a diamond on my ring finger,
after he left I carried that diamond in my purse.
I went by every pawnshop for six months,
parked in front of the buildings,
twirled the diamond in the sunlight and drove away.
Someone wanted to buy my ring
and propose to their girlfriend
but it didn't feel right
and everything felt out of place
and I think it's bad luck
but you can't tell people these things.

Some nights I sit up in bed
and close my eyes wondering
 what I'm doing with my life.
"You're someone," my best friend told me.
"You're beautiful"
Beauty doesn't matter to me
but you can't tell people these things.

Some days I feel like I'm living in a dream.
Some days I stare at myself in the

mirror lost in thought
but you can't tell dreams these things.

You can't tell people these things.

You can't tell people these things.

When we were eighteen we would make
videos of each other telling stupid jokes
and you would parade me around
saying, "Look here boys, this is love."
and everyone said we were too young
but we put our middle fingers to the sky and
said, "Shoot this bird down."
I know we never meant it.

The first time you held my hand
I felt like skipping stones across the Mississippi River.
I felt like taking off my clothes
and jumping into the cold ocean.
Jellyfish and all.
Sea turtles and all.

So tell me what you want.
So tell me what you need.
Tell me about that one time at band camp.
Tell me about how you hated college.
Tell me the stories I already know,
I want to relearn them a second time.
Let me touch that scar on your back
when you ask me to put sunscreen on you.

Ask me why I sleep with a heating blanket that
doesn't work.
Pick my heart up and throw it so far
that I swear I will hear you yelling,
"You were my first home run!"
Ask me why I put honey on my toast,
why the water runs cold too soon,
why I cry when I put flowers in a vase
because you once asked me why cut flowers

don't need sunlight
and I said, "They are already dying.

Sun can't bring them back."

Tell me why a love like ours can't come back to life,
why these years spent picking bad habits

off each other
turned into dry emails about finances.
Ask me the questions that used to make your heart
beat too fast.
Let me be the trophy

you never got when you played baseball.
Show me the places our ghosts danced from our
younger years.

Look me in the eyes and tell me you don't wonder
what my lips taste like now.
Look me in the eyes

and tell me it's been a year too long
since I've said your name followed behind mine.

$\mathscr{I}$used to be one of those women who valued a marriage proposal as the proudest moment of her life. I used to cut recipes out of magazines while cupcakes were baking in the oven. I used to be one of those women who could be found with curled hair and red lips pursed, delicately wrapped around the arm of man in a bow tie and glass of scotch in hand. I used to be that woman who sat outside at 3a.m. wondering where the excitement went, where her life went. I used to be one of those women who put on high heels and pearls while pretending to be the couple we were never *really* wanted to be.

I used to be one of those women who begged for a man to come back to her. I used to worry that if he wasn't there, my life would suddenly stop being there too.

He left and for one week I begged. Oh gosh, I begged. But what was I begging for? I woke up next to this man for years and watched him sleep. I only saw a white picket fence and a golden retriever. As he rested peacefully I saw my life, my adventure, my spirit drained of excitement. I loved him so much that I actually decided that I would live this way. I loved him so much that I thought if we weren't together, love would never find me again. Why was I begging for him back when he set me free? Why did I feel so....empty?

I used to be the woman who waited for adventure to find her. For months after he left I used to be the single woman who stared out windows while looking for a sign to get up and leave. It was right then, as I was sitting with wet hair dripping down my back and a towel wrapped around my chest, that I realized I had a choice.

I left. The college degree I had spent three years and twenty thousand dollars on seemed to fit me no better than a pair of shoes four sizes too small. I got a job that I loved, a job that made me excited about life. I started writing things down in a little black notebook. I ate organic food off delicate plates. I tucked myself into a bed with $300 sheets, silk blankets and pink pillows cases with ruffles.

I used to be that woman who begged for love, who waited for a man to tell her that she wasn't broken....but I wasn't broken. I became one of those women who had no room for a man because her car was full of flowers and pastries. I became one of those women that men don't know how to love because they just weren't quite sure where to put their hands, where to kiss. I became one of those women that men tried to capture and hold close...one of those women that slip through their fingers.

You see, I fell in love with life and the wind whispered,
"Why didn't you stay?
Why didn't you fight?"

I did fight.
I just didn't fight for him anymore.
I fought for me

I was never the little girl that
daydreamed about her wedding.
I daydreamed about going to college
and wearing red lipstick that stains coffee mugs.
I day dreamed of wearing diamond earrings
that I bought for myself
and living in a small apartment
filled with pink flowers.

Even when a ring was on my finger,
I was counting the ways to
back out of my vulnerability.
I tried on wedding dresses
and decided a white sundress
would suit me better.
I wanted to write literature
in the hems of my dress
and walk down the aisle with words in my hands,
not flowers.

The wedding never happened
and I replaced the ring on my finger
with the autobiography of Mark Twain.
It fit me better anyways
(and made me happier)

I still don't want a big wedding.
and I'd rather die than wear a silk wedding dress.
but I've healed enough
to imagine someone standing
at the end of that aisle again
and that's a step,
right?

Don't fall in love with someone who writes,
You will think each line is written about you.
Maybe it was
but maybe your laugh was just inspiration.

Don't fall in love with someone who writes,
you will never win the "I love you more" war
and your Valentine's Day cards will never compete.

Don't fall in love with someone who writes,
you will feel them tracing words on
your back as you sleep
and you will never understand
what those words mean.

But if you must fall in love with someone who writes,
and that writer loves you back,
you are one of the lucky ones:
your love will live forever,
stained on a paper
for the rest of time to read.

It's eight days into the new year,
and my foolish head has spent a week
thinking that the past wouldn't follow me here.

But the truth is
the past will pull up next to you at a stoplight,
make you lose your breath when the wind blows
in its scent.
You'll look up and see the past walking by you,
change lanes eight times
to stop seeing the past in your mirror.

You'll go home with shaking hands,
light a cigarette in the cold,
put it out because you're trying to quit.
make a cup of coffee,
sit cross legged in your bed,
breathe deep.

You keep moving, keep writing, keep smiling
until your new memories take the back seat
and maybe the past won't look like regret
but a chance to make it right.

If you said hello to me,
I'd say hello back.
If you asked me how I've been doing,
I'd say fine.
Just don't ask me if I've found love again
because I haven't even tried.
How could I tell you that I've
spent these months typing about you
while you found love
in someone else's words

and not mine.

She is a sunny day
when you had planned for a rainy one.
She is a poem that is well worded
with horrible grammar.
She is everything you hoped for
with a hint of unfamiliarity.

You will love her,
I assure you.

But I warn you now,
once you know someone like her exists
it will both bend and break your heart,
she is a love story with a twisted ending:

always waiting for love
but never needing to be saved.

When he calls me darlin'
my heart trips over his drawl.
He watches my lips kiss red lipstick at a stoplight
as I remind him to look
at the road while he's driving.
He rambles about how wine gives him a headache,
I leave a red kiss on his hand.

He thinks it's funny that I
keep oranges in the backseat
of my car.
He leaves the taste of citrus on
my lips when he says
fruit in the summer reminds him of being a kid.
Let me be your rekindled innocence,
climb my jungle gym all night long,
leave your sugary kisses on my wrists.
"Forbidden fruit," I say.

He says I'm the reason
the birds sing in the morning.
I tell him I'm the reason hurricanes
destroy innocent cities.
He's naive to the destruction love leaves behind.

Girls like me
are the reason people have storm shelters.
Boys like him
are the reason people forget to use them.

$\mathcal{I}$m a simple girl who makes picking out coffee creamer complicated. When I was a child I daydreamed about indigo kitchen tiles and wallpaper for my brick house of honeysuckle and lavender. I realized there are two types of people: the ones who drive with the windows down and the heater on high in the middle of winter and those who warm their hands by air vent at stoplights while the windows stay locked. I'm the person who rolls every damn window down and lets winter ride shotgun. I spend all of my money on candles and lemon heads. I like going grocery shopping alone, something about picking out bagels I never eat puts my mind at ease. I like how peaches make my lips sweet and sticky. I don't know why people think it's beautiful to be delicate. I'm a porcelain doll with glue kissed skin, I'm the freezer burn on your ice-cream. I don't know how to be fragile and made of steel at the same time.

I don't know how to be the sweet peach
with a core so sure and solid.

$\mathcal{P}$lease understand that I thrive off flowers that will one day wilt. I will save their broken petals and reminisce on lost beauty.

Please understand that I would rather be lost in my own head instead of trying to explain myself and hurt another's feelings.

Please understand that sometimes I am a loner and when these lonely times come, you may have to retrieve me.

Please understand that when you are falling asleep,
I am falling in love.

I fell asleep on my couch
watching old romance movies
with my glasses still on and my book in my hands.
I woke up and ate a spoon-full of frosting
and debated whether I should set the coffee maker
for the morning or not.

I have a king size bed with a blanket
on the end I never unfold.
I always sleep on the left side,
the right side kept perfectly made.
Some nights my room is so quiet
that I can hear my heartbeat.
Quiet is something I've had to get used to.

I bought a glass bottle of root beer today
and couldn't get the cap off,
this man gently took it out of my hands,
opened it, smiled and walked away.

I was talking to my friends
about how I want to find love,
honestly I'm not sure that I really do.

Unless it's someone that will laugh
as I struggle to open
a glass bottle of root beer
and instead of opening it for me he says,
"You can do it, I know you can."

PART 3

You keep moving, keep writing, keep smiling until
your new memories take the front seat and maybe
your past won't look like regret
but a chance to make things right.

Whispering Bones

*D*ear me
when you wake up
and forget how to look at the world with warmth,
when it takes all of the energy you have
to turn off the alarm and open the blinds:
remember this.

When you look in the mirror
and see your stretches coming back,
the vitamins you take every morning,
the medicine in your purse
when you can't breathe
because you had that dream again
and you can't think straight
because you feel like world is caving in:
remember this.

When you can't sleep and stare at the ceiling,
playing your past like a projection movie
lit by the glow of your phone,
When you feel like your wings were clipped too short
When you've gone months without writing anything:
remember this.

Remember that you may still be young
but your bones have held you so strong.
Please don't ever let them stop whispering,
please remember this:
You are stronger than this.
You deserve more than this.
You fought the war before it began
and you'll celebrate the victory long before it's over.
You are
my
hero.

On the day that I meet the man I'm going to marry
I will probably sleep past my alarm,
trip over my shoes out the door,
and stop at the grocery store on the way to work
because I forgot that today is my day to bring
breakfast. He'll be there picking out fruit or cereal
and when he says hello, I'll just look at him and say,
"I'm really sorry you have to meet me this way."
as I try to fix my hair and adjust my shirt.
We'll probably exchange numbers and
drink coffee at some shitty diner the following night.
We'll laugh about how we met,
Me running into him as I turned an aisle too quick.
He'll tell me that there is something different about
me, he'll notice how I hold my coffee,
how I stare into space and swear I'm paying
attention. He'll probably notice right off the bat
that I have a hard time sitting still
and mid-sentence I'll interrupt him to say,
"Let's go buy a tent. Let's camp outside tonight."
I'll notice how he looks at me with curiosity,
how his eyes grow big when I answer in excitement,
I keep track of how many times he fidgets with his
watch, I note that he doesn't like too much cream in
his coffee, I chip in that I like a little coffee with my
cream. I'll look back at him and smile
when he asks if I too have been looking
in all the wrong places for someone
just like him.

*he probably was expecting someone graceful
and elegant
but he'll grow to love how hard I tripped and fell in
love with him.*

A letter to myself:

So what, you skipped lunch with a friend to dust your coffee table and clean your sheets. So what. You aren't the only person in the world who has taken a shower with plans to go out but end up changing your mind when you look in the mirror and think, "I'm tired. I want to sit here and write tonight."

You feel like the people who dial the wrong number and call you might actually have something to say. Like the time some lady in Ohio accidentally left a voicemail on your phone saying, "Happy Birthday, Trish. I hope God blesses you today." Remember when you called that lady back and said, "I'm not Trish but you have no idea how much I needed to hear that." You aren't the calls that you ignore, you aren't the calls that never came. You aren't somebody's second choice, their "go to", their "maybe in the future we can try." Turn off your phone.

You are more than your favorite dress. You are more than the body you try to hide, the stretch marks on your hips. You have no self-confidence and I don't know why. Maybe because people tell you all the time how beautiful you are and you are the only person in this damn world that doesn't see it. If you could see yourself smile I swear you'd believe it.

You spend too much time waiting for the future, thinking that when you get the degree, when the seasons change, when you get that promotion your life will begin. You stupid girl, you've wasted a year waiting for life to begin. You naïve, beautiful thing, you've wasted so many minutes dreaming about life that you haven't given yourself a minute to open the front door, leave your house and fucking live it.

*A*nyone who has ever walked out of my life,
I fought for until I was sending my love
to empty mailboxes just to say,
"I know you don't stop by anymore
but I swear I think of you every day."
And I know that it is hard to drink coffee over tears
but this heart, these fragile wrists, this tear soaked
pillow, will always hand you every ounce of courage
they have left.
Please listen when I tell you
that this poetry is my testimony to the fight in my
heart. Please listen when I tell you
that you may not recognize the person that I am now
but look how far I've walked on bloody knees just to
come to your door and say,
"You better believe I will stand here every day"
and when they say, "Just put a smile on"
it's okay to say 'fuck you' over heavy breathing.
and I won't sugarcoat the truth:
This may just be the beginning of the storm
and you may feel like you can't weather anymore,
you may see the tsunami coming,
and feel like you've already been drowning for a year
but you keep fighting, do you hear me?
You may feel like the levees in New Orleans,
You may break and flood the city in your soul
but I promise you even lakes evaporate
when the sun shines for days
and that river of sadness flowing through your veins
will not flow forever.
The next time someone tells you that
you are too much soul,
give them a smile and cry if you need to
but don't you give up.
You've come so far.

You grabbed my hand and begged me to stay.
my hair was blowing in the wind
and I couldn't hear the truth in your words
over the sound of the waves pulling me out to sea.
Sweetheart, I've been gone.
Sweetheart, I've been gone.
Maybe you find yourself farthest
from where you've been.
Maybe who you are is waiting at the other end.
I never looked back.
I was made for this.

Walk away from everything you've ever known.
I swear the view is beautiful.

This afternoon I was writing down a few things I needed from the store in an old notebook. I flipped the page to continue my list when I stumbled across a note I had written to myself:

Dear you,
One day you may feel lost and one day you may forget who you are but please remember these things:
-You are your own responsibility
-There is nothing scary in your room, go to sleep
-Happiness can be found in clean sheets
-But remember cheap laundry detergent sucks
-Cold air feels good in your lungs, breathe deep
-Remember to adventure
-You first, always
-You alone are your future
-The sun will always rise, even on a rainy day
-Open your blinds and tie back your curtains
-"We've only just started this party"
-Take a walk even if you don't know where you are going
-The sun will always burn your skin. (I swear if you mess up our skin I will be so mad at you. Wear sunscreen!)
-Stop buying bagels, you never eat them
-Think deep and find beauty in the little things
-I told you he wasn't the one

Taped to the back was a $20 bill and sloppy cursive, "I bet your gas light is on."

Signed August 2011

When you turn thirteen
and want to paint your nails black
I'll rummage through an old drawer
and give you my own polish.
When you look at me and say, "Momma, I'm lost."
I'll turn you towards the mirror
and say, "Run darlin', don't ever let them find you."
When the first day of high school comes
and you hurry to get out of the car
with nerves in hand
 I'll tell you,
"Don't run, walk slow. You'll make it through."
You'll make it through.
One day that boy will break your heart
and when you lock yourself in your room
I'll buy you a journal, a brand new pen,
a 2 liter of strawberry soda
and a potted violet with a note saying something like,
"White oleanders are poisonous and so is heartache.
Violets symbolize something
that long I've since forgotten
and strawberry soda drowns the salt in your tears."
This. Remember this.
Remember how far you've come.
Believe in petunias.
You may look at a petunia, burnt and weeping
and feel sorry for it, thinking it dead
but if you trim off the fading flowers
you will see it gasp for fresh air, growing back to life.
Cut off your dead flowers,
tilt your broken limbs towards the sun
and when the rain comes dance with the roses.
You'll marry young or maybe old.
You'll have a daughter of your own
and watch the sun rise in her eyes

and when she looks at you with tears in her eyes
saying, "Momma, I'm lost."
turn her towards the mirror
and say, "Run darlin', don't ever let them find you."

Remember the white oleanders
Remember how their poison makes them beautiful.

I swear the past month has passed before me while I've just stood here burning holes in my paper and my scarves. I tried listening to one of those videos that talk you into a relaxed state while you listen to birds chipping. I just sat there with my legs crossed trying to stop thinking about Christmas lights.

Yep. Christmas lights. Where should I put them? What color should I buy? Honestly, they are the only thing that feels familiar. I wake up some mornings and blink twice thinking, "Where the hell am I?" These walls need to be painted and my closet is too big for just my clothes. I trip over the same extension cord every damn day.

I bought Christmas lights tonight, by the way. White is the color I decided on after standing in the aisle for twenty minutes. When I got home I plugged them in and only half the strand worked. Figures, right? The only thing I can think straight about doesn't even know how to think straight. Regardless, I put them up outside my front door. After struggling with them for ten minutes, I admired my half-lit string of lights and thought in regards to my life, "hang me up as I am...confused, tired, restless but fucking beautiful."

I've held the door open
for so many strangers that my eyes hardly
recognize the loved ones I've slammed the door on.
There are days that I look out the window
and feel a pain in my chest
because I don't remember how I got here.
The truth is,
I can't save you.
I can't stop you from drowning in your own head
and I can't pull you from the sea.
But I can build a home that is safe from the world,
a place where you look out every window
and see your name in the wind.
We can climb the tallest tree
to watch the sun set on the world we forgot to see.
You may turn to thank me
and realize I was never there at all:
You found the strength to rebuild all by yourself.
That's the love I want.

My mind is diseased.
My eyes are blinded.
My words are twisted
by love.
The rare love.
The kind of love that pricks your finger with passion
and your world changes
like plugging in your Christmas tree for the first time.
The kind of love that makes your head spin
with addicting dizziness.
The kind of love that sends a shock
up your spine when you realize
this is what you've been waiting for.
And I'm not much interested in anything
but that kind of love.
(Even if it means I'll only ever write about it)

Fall in love with a woman who writes.
Let her tell you she loves you
in a million different ways.
Let her type your voice into every poem.
When you hear the clicks
of her keyboard late at night,
remember that is her dreaming:
She dreams when she writes, not when she sleeps.

Fall in love with a woman who writes.
Know that she has memorized
the way your eyes display sadness.
Know that your touch is her inspiration.
Be patient when she cries over lost love
and stories with no ending.

Fall in love with a woman who writes.
Let her tell you of her past,
handing you her tattered book of secrets.
Pay attention to every sentence underlined.
Kiss her hands
and ignore the ink smudged on her palms.

Fall in love with a woman who writes.
There may be quiet nights.
There may be words you'll never understand.
But be patient,
you are the love story she's been waiting to write.

These are my words.
This is my hurt,
Here is my happiness.
I wear my soul on my fingertips
and invite strangers to come by
and take a piece home.
I don't need all of this soul,
I'm too many lifetimes in one person.

These are my veins.
They've pushed me through the toughest times.
They've pumped more courage
into my heart than blood.
They've held my strength together
when my bones wanted to crumble.
I asked the night sky how it stays so calm
I asked where it found those stars
and the moon wept,
"The sun.
The sun needs to breathe.
She needs to rest."
The moon loves the sun and the sun loves the moon
but they are never in the same place at the same time
and I think my soul is a lot like this.
I think my words twinkle all of the sad stories
while my body tries to create happy memories.
I think my words carry my burdens
and my body moves in laughs.
I hope my words and my body one day meet
so I can sleep without them keeping me up at night
trying to contact each other to say,
"This is enough.
She needs to breathe.
She needs to rest."

 I'm not a writer.
I'm a hopeless romantic
bleeding out my past
like a poison
so I can be cured
of my illness
before love
finds me again.

You told me you wished
you could sleep in my thoughts
so maybe you could understand
why I cry when I'm happy,
why I could never finish a book
without skipping a few pages,
why I could never stop falling in love
with words lasting in heartache.

You told me you wished
you could sleep in my thoughts
so maybe you could find a way
to make me love you half
as much as I loved the words
you could never say.

But I loved the way your name sounded.
You spoke in cursive,
You never needed beautiful words.

Sometimes I feel like I'm the broken girl,
The one who writes in pink ink
and has burn holes in her dresses.
Sometimes I feel like I'm the broken girl,
the girl who fixed herself the best she could.
And sometimes the stitches come unglued
and sometimes my heart beats too fast
when it shouldn't
but I'm happy.
Look, I know I'm not always beautiful.
My nails are always chipped
and my hands shake when I drive
but I have a lot of love to give.
I know sometimes I feel like the broken girl,
but my love isn't broken.
It's the only wholeness I've ever known.

They say it hurt
because it mattered
but maybe it hurt
because it didn't matter
and it should have.

Don't listen to a word your head tells you,
it doesn't know what it's talking about.
I've learned that what makes the most sense
are the experiences that make no sense at all.
I've learned that the thoughts your mind
propels through you late at night
are generated by your fears.

Remember those fears.
Do every single thing
that scares the hell out of you.
Don't think twice.

Someone once told me to be scared
Is a good thing.

I think that's true.

One day you'll love someone
so much that it will hurt.
This love will cripple you
until it breaks your heart.
It won't be your fault,
you gave away more passion than returned.

One day you'll wake up
and feel a thousand knives in your back,
you will curse love
until you realize it wasn't love's fault,
You left your heart in reckless hands,
you took a gamble.
It's okay.

Your wounds will heal,
;ove will call your name again.

One day you'll love someone
so much and it won't hurt.

One day you'll love someone
so much that 'love' isn't a big enough word.

There were days spent planning for the future that I nearly forgot I was living right here, right now. I nearly forgot that if I don't learn how to fight back soon, my plans will leave me in an alley all alone.

I sat here for three weeks.
Three weeks wondering when my hands would stop shaking. Three weeks wondering when my back would stop bleeding. For three weeks I was bound to the realities of one more failure. I was bound to one more moving box saying,
"All those plans I made...
Yeah, they didn't work out."

I spent four months wondering if I changed my appearance maybe my past wouldn't recognize me, maybe my past wouldn't find me. I spent four months lining my eyes with expensive mascara, the kind that wouldn't run down my cheeks when I realized daily that I didn't know what the hell my future contained.

I don't know where I'm going with this.
I don't know exactly what I'm trying to say
except that I'm okay now.
I don't need to be saved.
I found myself in the room where my thirteen
year old self wrote 'love'
on the front of a notebook.

I'm okay now.
I don't need to be saved.

Some nights my wrists ache
from tracing the same sentence onto this page:

I would love you for all my life,
if I could just find where you are.

*C*losure.

It will drift in from your window,
a tablespoon every night.
mixing with your dreams
without a hint of its presence
until one morning you wake up
without that name in your mouth.
you open the blinds
and the sun shines on the dust
that settled on your heart.
Those wasted months you spent in the dark
will seem distant and blurry.
You will take a deep breath
and say hello
to the you that was there all along,
patiently waiting for your heartache
to show you your strength.

He said he didn't want
anything to do with me anymore
because he already 'paid me off',
It made me wonder if when I pay off my student
loans, my degree will have no longer have value
either.

I have to get my tonsils removed.
I know I've talked circles
about the one who walked away
but I feel like he was a piece of me
that I didn't really need,
that caused me so much pain
and for some reason I put off removing.
Apparently the surgery is worse on adults,
apparently the recovery process is hell
but my doctor says I'll live a better life
if I just face the facts and do it.

I imagine that I cried when I lost my first tooth,
I imagine that I didn't understand why
I didn't need it anymore.
I never wanted to lose my innocence,
I never wanted to remove the pieces of my body
that my mother grew for me.

My brother told me that everybody has to die
as he looked at his garden.
He said we are orcas. I laughed until he got quiet
and said we are orcas because he knows that
his daughter will have always have a family
if ever he is gone.
They say an entire orca pod stays together for life,
they say each pod has its own dialect
and language.

They say orcas have a larger part of their brain
for emotions than humans,
that the mother will sometimes carry
her deceased child in her mouth for a week
before letting them go.
My brother is 31 and is in kidney failure
I wonder if he has spent more time
thinking about the flowers at his funeral
than the flowers at his daughter's wedding.
I don't want to admit this,
I don't want to think about this
but I can't ignore it either.

If I could stand in your driveway
with my tears in a jar and my happiness in
another, I swear I'd hand you every smile I had left
in me, I swear I'd give you every laugh for the rest
of my life.
Even when we hit our funny bone,
we wince while everyone else laughs.
I'd slam myself into the corner of every table
just to see you smile.

I've spent too many nights trying to write poems
to the wounded, hoping my words can heal
someone. You say that it's too hard to watch me
self-destruct. Tonight I wonder
if I should have written those poems to myself.
But my life is an open book, you see.
Life hurts and life isn't fair
but I can't pretend sadness isn't bittersweet
when you of all people know
that even the caterpillars weep when their friend
becomes a butterfly before they are ready
to say
goodbye.

Time.
Punishes you.
Scares you.
Rushes you.

"Time heals all wounds."
I always hated that saying
until I looked in the mirror
and my wounds
were now battle scars.

Time.
Blesses you.

Dear me,

I hope you wake up one day and feel more alive than ever. I hope you have a day off where you do nothing but drink coffee and listen to your favorite songs. I hope that you stop waiting for a sign before your life passes you by. (just go do it) I hope you drink a margarita under a palm tree and laugh until you cry. I hope you will put down your pen for one day and think of something else other than words. I hope you travel. Please, just wake up and leave. And when you leave, I hope you fall in love with life again. I hope you remember your past with a smile on your face. All I ever wanted was for you to be happy.

Sincerely,
Me

The scariest thing I have ever done is currently in your hands. There is nothing more terrifying than sending your diary into the world. I never intended to write a book. I began sharing my writing on a blog that had one follower, my sister. It truly grew into something I never, ever expected. I would like to thank every single one of my followers on that blog, because of your support this book was brought to life.

Please feel free to reread this book a second time with a different outlook in mind. I challenge you to go through it with a highlighter. Bend the pages, draw in the margins, make a grocery list on the back of this page. I love writing in my books. I suppose I feel this way because that book made a mark on my life and honestly it only feels appropriate to return the favor.

Drew

Cover photo by B. Spinola
I love you more
than coconut cake.

CPSIA information can be obtained at www.ICGtesting.com
Printed in the USA
LVOW08s1529050415

433367LV00032B/934/P